"Having known Lawrence Shapiro for more than twenty years as a highly innovative and prolific producer of therapeutic workbooks, I am proud to endorse his new edition of *The ADHD Workbook for Kids*, as an excellent resource for therapists and families."

—**Hugh Kingsley, (MEd research),** president of The Brainary LLC

"Lawrence Shapiro's vast experience and knowledge make this book a must-have for anyone working with attention-deficit/hyperactivity disorder (ADHD) children and teens. *The ADHD Workbook for Kids* gives easy-to-follow strategies to help children with ADHD build essential life skills. This is one of the most useful tools I have seen for parents, as well as professionals."

—**Marta Perez, PhD, JD,** former Miami-Dade County Public Schools board member, and dedicated advocate for student success and educational excellence

"Lawrence Shapiro speaks to kids in a language they can understand. The workbook is full of creative and engaging activities to help children with executive functions, perspective taking, and managing their behaviors and emotions."

—**Randy Kulman, PhD,** director of Digitally Nutritious

"I've referred clients to Lawrence Shapiro's books for decades and will add this one to the list. I'm especially happy to see advice for parents along with activities which include them, as parental involvement is a critical part of any child's emotional health program. The games and activities—from puzzles to breathwork—cover all bases for teaching comprehensive ADHD life skills while keeping the reader's attention along the way!"

—**Lisa M. Schab, LCSW,** practicing psychotherapist; and author of more than twenty self-help books, including *Put Your Worries Here* and *Put Your Feelings Here*

The ADHD Workbook for Kids

Second Edition

Helping Children Gain Self-Confidence, Social Skills & Self-Control

Lawrence E. Shapiro, PhD

Instant Help Books
An Imprint of New Harbinger Publications, Inc.

Publisher's Note

This publication is designed to provide accurate and authoritative information in regard to the subject matter covered. It is sold with the understanding that the publisher is not engaged in rendering psychological, financial, legal, or other professional services. If expert assistance or counseling is needed, the services of a competent professional should be sought.

INSTANT HELP, the Clock Logo, and NEW HARBINGER are trademarks of New Harbinger Publications, Inc.

Distributed in Canada by Raincoast Books

Copyright © 2025 by Lawrence E. Shapiro
Instant Help Books
An imprint of New Harbinger Publications, Inc.
5720 Shattuck Avenue
Oakland, CA 94609
www.newharbinger.com

Cover design by Sara Christian

Interior book design by Tom Comitta

Acquired by Tesilya Hanauer

Edited by Joyce Wu

All Rights Reserved

Printed in the United States of America

27 26 25
10 9 8 7 6 5 4 3 2 1   First Printing

CONTENTS

Dear Parents		6
Letter to Kids		8

Part 1: It's Great to Be Good

1	Catch Me Being Good	11
2	The Kindness Jar	15
3	Rules and Consequences	16
4	How Your Behavior Affects Others	20
5	The Gift of Caring Words	22
6	How Can You Help?	24
7	Good Manners	26
8	Understanding Instructions	28
9	Dealing with Distractions	30
10	You Can Be Patient	31

Part 2: All Feelings Are Okay — It's What You Do With Them That Counts

11	The Anger Thermometer	37
12	Talking About Your Feelings	40
13	Practice Being Mindful	43
14	Creating a Quiet Place	45
15	Shape Breathing	46

16	When You Have Difficult Feelings	48
17	Where Do Your Feelings Come From?	51
18	Understanding How Others Feel	54
19	More Than One Feeling at a Time	57
20	Things That Are Great About You!	61

Part 3: Changing Your Brain

21	Thinking Ahead	65
22	Organizing Your Work	68
23	Paying Attention to Time	70
24	My Weekly Goals	74
25	Making Good Choices	76
26	Remembering What Comes Next	78
27	Making a Plan	82
28	Learning to Be Patient	86
29	Keep Trying Even If It's Hard	88

Part 4: How to Make and Keep Good Friends

30	How to Find Good Friends	97
31	Making Time for Friends	101
32	Learning to Cooperate	102
33	You Can Be a Leader	105
34	Be a Humor Detective	108

35	Joining Others at Play	111
36	Solving Conflicts with Others	113
37	Understanding What Others Think and Feel	116
38	Understanding Personal Space	120

Part 5: Making the Most Out of School

39	Asking for Help with Your Schoolwork	125
40	Using Notes to Remember Important Things to Do	127
41	Knowing When to Take a Break	129
42	Using Technology to Help with Your ADHD	130
43	Completing Homework Assignments	133
44	Preparing for a Test	136
45	Speaking in Front of the Class	139
46	Following Directions in School	142
47	Hidden Rules at School	144
48	The Gifts of ADHD	147
Answer Key		151

Dear Parents

I've been working with children with ADHD for over 40 years. Over that time, I've learned what to prioritize in helping these fun, creative, and yes, often challenging children.

This workbook is divided into 5 sections:

1. **It's Great to Be Good**
   This section teaches children the importance of good behavior.

2. **All Feelings Are Okay—It's What You Do with Them That Counts**
   This section teaches children the importance of emotional regulation. Emotional regulation means the ability to identify and communicate feelings, tolerate uncomfortable feelings, and express feelings in appropriate ways.

3. **Changing Your Brain**
   This section is focused on the difficulties children with ADHD have with executive functioning, which includes such skills as being on time, planning ahead, problem solving, and organizing their work.

4. **How to Make and Keep Good Friends**
   Kids with ADHD often have problems making and keeping friends. This section teaches children a variety of social skills to help them with their social development.

5. **Making the Most out of School**
   Many children with ADHD, while bright and creative, fall behind at school. This section focuses on the skills that will help bring academic success.

There are lots of different kinds of activities in this workbook, including a game to play in each section. I encourage you to sit with your child when they're working through this book. Doing these focused activities with your child will help you understand how they think and feel, give you opportunities to model appropriate behaviors, and give positive reinforcement as your child learns new social, emotional, and behavioral skills.

Most of all, working and playing with your child will help you build a strong relationship. Child psychologists emphasize that spending just 10 or 15 minutes a day in child-centered activities (what we sometimes call "special time") will help your child develop self-confidence and a sense of purpose as they meet the challenges ahead.

Some of the activities in this workbook require cutting and pasting. If you do not want to take pages from the book, you can go to **http://www.newharbinger. com/56029** to print out copies of this material. When I mention something in the book that you'll also find in the free tools, I'll indicate this on the page too.

There are no simple answers for children with ADHD, and every child has unique needs. But it's my hope that with patient guidance and good support, your child will achieve the happiness and success that we all wish for our children.

Sincerely,

Lawrence E. Shapiro, PhD

Letter to Kids

What's it like for you to have ADHD? I've known lots of kids with ADHD, and they tell me it's not really a problem most of the time, but sometimes it's really frustrating.

Kids with ADHD tell me that they get into trouble more often than other kids do. They tell me that their teachers and parents are always saying things like "I know you can do better if you just try a little harder," even when they've tried very hard in the first place! Most kids with ADHD tell me that they don't have many friends and that sometimes their classmates are mean to them.

This workbook will help you with the challenges that can come along with having ADHD. Each activity will teach you a new skill. You'll learn to handle a different part of your ADHD a little better, and you'll also have some fun while you learn. I've included lots of activities that kids enjoy, like drawing and mazes and games.

But I wouldn't be honest if I said that these activities don't require some work too. And the more you work, the more you will learn about yourself and your ADHD.

Some activities you will be able to do yourself, and some may require help from your parents, caregivers, or teachers. If you have a counselor, they'll probably want to help you with these activities too. Don't be afraid to ask for help when you need it.

There are lots of people who want to help you be happy, healthy, and successful every day of your life—and I'm one of them!

Best of luck,

Dr. Larry

Part 1
It's Great to Be Good

Catch Me Being Good

It's always important to be good. But what does that really mean? Good behavior means following rules, helping others, being patient, being respectful and kind, and so much more. This activity will help you think about the importance of being good.

Begin by coloring in the 4 pictures of good behavior on this page.

Be polite when talking on the phone.

Help with pets.

Brush your teeth and wash up without being asked.

Do quiet activities by yourself.

Now, draw 4 pictures of yourself doing good behaviors. Write down what you are doing under each picture. You can ask a parent or teacher to help you if you are not sure about which behaviors are most important to them.

Finally, ask your parents if they will play the Catch Me Being Good Game with you. Cut out the "catch me being good" coupons, **which an adult can help you print out at http://www.newharbinger.com/56029**. Ask your parents to give you a coupon when they catch you doing the 4 behaviors you have drawn. See how long it takes you to collect 10 coupons.

Print this page at
http://www.newharbinger.com/56029

The Kindness Jar

It's always a good idea to be kind. Everyone loves kids (and adults too) who are kind. There are so many ways to be kind. You can send someone a get well card. You can hold the door for someone. You can give someone a compliment, like "That's a pretty dress, Mom!"

Write as many kind things you can do in the kindness jar below, and put a circle around the act of kindness when you do it.

Maybe you can make a kindness jar for the whole family? Just get a plastic jar or container and ask people to put in a coin for each time someone in the house experiences something kind from someone else. Maybe if you get enough coins, you can all go out and get a kindness treat! I'd vote for ice cream—how about you?

Rules and Consequences

How many rules do you have in your life? I bet sometimes it feels like there are a million rules! There are probably not a million rules, but I bet there are quite a lot.

Here are some rules you probably have to follow:

- Eat with your mouth closed.

- Go to bed without a fuss.

- Always say "thank you" when someone does something nice for you.

- Look both ways before crossing a street.

And what happens if you don't follow these rules? When you don't follow rules, there are consequences.

Consequences are the result of your actions, good or bad. If you don't brush your teeth, you'll probably get cavities. If you do brush your teeth, you'll have healthy teeth and gums. When you don't follow rules, the consequences are not going to be good ones because ignoring even small rules have consequences.

In the space below, write in what happened to these kids who broke the rules:

Theo talked loudly in the movie theater. **What do you think happened?**

_____

_____

Tiffany got a new bike for her birthday from her grandmother, but didn't say "thank you." **What do you think happened?**

_____
_____
_____

Tyler's dad told him to go to bed, but Tyler said, "You can't make me go to bed if I'm not tired." **What do you think happened?**

_____
_____
_____

Write down three rules that are important in your home.

_____
_____
_____

Write down three rules that are important in your school.

_____
_____
_____

Now it's your turn to think about rules and consequences with a fun game.

You can play this game with a friend or family member, and it will get you thinking more about rules and their consequences and why following rules is so important.

THE RULES AND CONSEQUENCES GAME

Number of players: 2

What you need to play:

- The Game Board

- 10 pennies

- 10 nickels or quarters

Instructions:

1. Lay the game board page as flat as you can. **(You can also print out a copy of the game board by going to http://www.newharbinger. com/56029.)**

2. Each player takes 10 coins (one person gets the pennies, the other gets the nickels or quarters).

3. The younger player tosses a coin so that it lands on the game board. Then, they must describe a rule and a consequence of breaking it in the place where the coin lands. For example, if a coin lands on the square with a kitchen, the player might say, "A rule is 'Don't touch a hot stove.' The consequence is 'If you touch a hot stove, you might burn yourself.'"

4. Then, the next player goes, tossing a coin and describing a rule and consequence.

5. If you miss the board, then the next player takes a turn.

6. When all the coins are used, count up the number of coins each player has on the board. If a player gets 3 coins in a row on the board (vertically, horizontally, or diagonally), then they get 3 bonus points. The player with the most points wins.

18

How Your Behavior Affects Others

People judge you by the way you treat others. If you are friendly, helpful, and caring, people will appreciate it and want to be with you. If you hit your friends or refuse to play by the rules of a game, people won't like it and probably won't want to be with you.

Learning how your behavior affects others can help you follow rules when you need to. It can also help you find and make friends.

In the picture below, the children are acting in different ways. Put a circle around the kids who are acting kindly and an X over the kids who are not.

Now, ask a parent or caregiver, a sibling, or a friend:

What is the nicest thing someone has done for you? What happened?

What is something unkind someone has done to you? What happened?

What have you learned about what it means to act kindly and unkindly?

Is there anything you might want to change about the way you behave, to act more kindly to others?

ACTIVITY 5: The Gift of Caring Words

Caring words are great gifts. And they are so easy to give!

The girl below is named Shania. She's sad because her grandmother is very sick. Can you circle the gifts that show caring words that might help Shania feel better?

Now, go back and color in the gifts that you would give Shania.

Could you give the gift of caring words to someone today? **Below, write down what you could say to them.**

Do you want to tell me about it?

I'll listen if you want to talk.

Stop that stupid crying.

Stop your whining.

Can I help you?

Would you like to be alone?

How Can You Help?

There are so many ways you can help others. Below are some helping superheroes. Each has a special power.

Read the following statements about people who need help. Draw a line from each statement to the superhero who might be most helpful. (There may be a couple right answers.)

Don had some boxes he wanted flattened.

Judy couldn't reach a can on the top cupboard.

Khalid wanted someone to go running with him.

Journee was lonely and wanted a best friend.

Keisha wanted to hang a picture and needed someone to poke a hole in the wall.

See Answer Key on page 151.

WHAT IS YOUR HELPING SUPERPOWER?

Draw your face on the helping superhero below. You could also paste in a photo of yourself.

Draw in objects around the figure that show others your helping superpower.

ACTIVITY 7

Good Manners

It's important to have good manners when you eat. Nate had terrible manners. What do you think other kids would say to Nate about his manners? What do you think will happen if Nate eats like this in a restaurant or school lunchroom? **In the spaces below, write the problems you see with Nate's manners (or other types of bad manners).** You'll see an example to get you started.

Eating with his hands.

See Answer Key on page 151.

Do you also struggle with manners sometimes?

Sometimes it can be hard to remember to do things like cleaning up or waiting our turn to talk. There's so much else we want to do! But good manners are a way to show other people you care.

What are some ways Nate could improve his manners? What are some ways you could improve your manners too?

Understanding Instructions

Sometimes when you're listening to directions, you might not understand everything you're told. When that happens, it's important to ask for help so you can be sure to get the instructions right.

The children in the pictures below need help understanding directions. **Choose one of the phrases at the bottom of the page to write in their conversation balloons, so they know what to say to ask for help.** (There may be more than one correct answer—choose the one that feels comfortable for you.)

See Answer Key on page 151.

Could you please repeat that?

I don't understand what you said.

Could you explain what that means?

Once again, please.

This is hard to understand. Could you please tell me again in different words?

Dealing with Distractions

It's hard to focus on what you're doing if other things take away your attention. One way to make focusing easier is to eliminate as many distractions in your environment as you can.

Lorissa is having a hard time trying to study for her math test because there are so many distractions in the room. **List the distractions on the lines below. See if you can find all 10.**

_____

_____

_____

_____

See Answer Key on page 151.

You Can Be Patient

Have you ever had someone ask you "Can't you just sit still and be patient?" Most kids with ADHD hear this a lot, but nobody can be patient all the time. Many adults have a hard time waiting. Maybe you've been in a traffic jam where people are honking at each other and even yelling out the window. Or maybe you've seen an adult get angry at a computer that was running slowly.

Most people don't like to wait for things, but some things can't be rushed. Here are 5 things that can't be rushed:

- Growing up
- Your birthday
- A visit to the doctor's office
- Learning to play a sport or an instrument
- A garden

Can you think of 5 more times you need to be patient because things just can't be rushed?

_____
_____
_____
_____

CREATE A PATIENCE BOX

A Patience Box can help when it seems that time is going really slowly and there's nothing you can do about it.

Ask an adult for a shoebox, and decorate it if you like. On the next page, write down 10 things you can do to help you be patient. For example, you might write "Make a sculpture out of clay" or "Work on a Lego project." Then, cut them out and put them in your Patience Box.

You can ask adults or even your friends to write down some interesting activities too.

The next time you have a hard time being patient, close your eyes and reach into your Patience Box. Pick up to 3 activities to do, and then choose the one that you think would be most fun.

Part 2
All Feelings Are Okay—
It's What You Do With Them That Counts

The Anger Thermometer

Do you get angry very often? What are the top three things that make you angry? **Write them below:**

1. _____
2. _____
3. _____

Take a look at this list of 10 ways to calm yourself down when you're frustrated and angry. Circle the ones that you think will work for you:

- Deep breathing: Take a deep, slow breath in through your nose, hold it for the count of 5, and then let it out slowly through your mouth. Do this 5 more times.

- Imagine a peaceful place: Close your eyes and think of your favorite quiet place, like a beach, a park, or even somewhere in your house. Imagine you're there, and everything feels peaceful and happy.

- Count to 10: When you feel really angry, start counting slowly from 1 to 10. By the time you reach 10, you might feel a little less angry.

- Squeeze a stress ball: If you have a squishy ball or a soft toy, give it a good squeeze. Hold your squeeze and count to 30.

- Draw or scribble: Grab some paper and crayons, and draw or scribble whatever you feel like.

- Talk to a grown-up: Find a grown-up you trust, like a parent or teacher, and tell them what's bothering you. Talking about your feelings can help a lot.

- Take a break: If you can, walk away from what's making you mad and find a quiet place to cool down. If this happens in the classroom, ask your teacher if it's okay to take this kind of break.

- Use a fidget toy: If you have a fidget toy, like a spinner, playing with it can help distract your mind and calm your feelings. Try breathing deeply while you do this.

- Listen to music: Put on your favorite song, especially one that makes you feel happy or relaxed. Music can quickly help you change your mood.

- Jump around or dance: Sometimes moving your body can help get rid of the angry energy. You can jump, dance, or even run in place.

- Hug a stuffed animal: Wrap your arms around your favorite stuffed animal and hold it tight until you feel yourself start to calm down.

Now, try this to see how these ideas work:

Sit back in a chair and think of the last time you were really angry. Think about it until you start to feel a little angry again.

Point to the place on the anger thermometer below that shows how you feel. The higher up on the thermometer you point, the angrier you are.

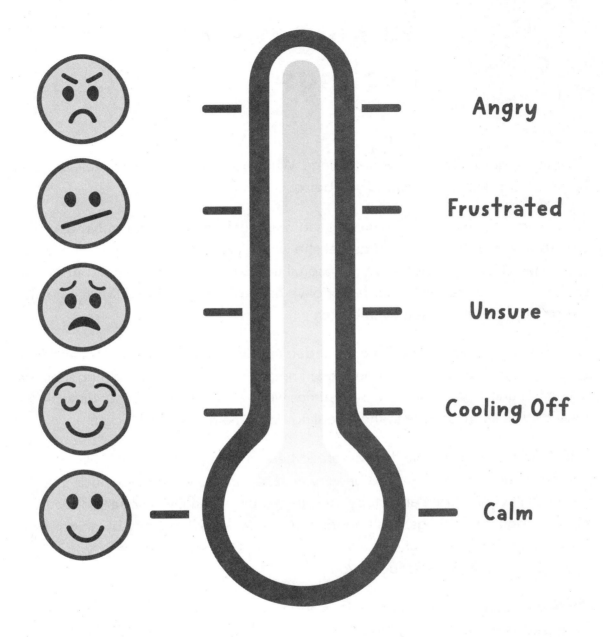

Now, look at the first anger technique you circled and give it a try. Use the anger thermometer again. Did your "anger temperature" go down?

The next time you feel really angry, do this again. Try one of the anger control techniques, and use the anger thermometer to see how well it works. If it doesn't work well, try another technique!

Talking About Your Feelings

It's important to talk about your feelings. When you talk about your feelings, it helps other people understand you better.

Take Deidre, for example. Deidre felt sad one morning. When her father asked Deidre what was wrong, she said that she was thinking about her grandma, who was very sick and had gone to the hospital the day before. Deidre felt better after sharing her feelings. When her father gave her a big hug and said they could visit her grandma later, she felt even better.

Talking about feelings helps people understand you. When they understand you, they can give you help if you need it. Sharing can also prevent upsetting feelings from affecting your whole day. Sometimes when you don't talk about upsetting feelings, like sadness or fear, those feelings become bigger and bigger.

Take Dwayne, for example. He was afraid he was going to flunk his spelling test, and he thought his mom would be very mad at him. He worried so much that he couldn't concentrate and study for the test! But when Dwayne talked to his mother about his feelings, she understood. She helped him study by going over his spelling words again and again. And she told Dwayne, "As long as you do your best, I'll always be proud of you."

The more you talk about your feelings and hear other people talk about their feelings, the more you'll understand your feelings and other people's. You'll have what we call "emotional intelligence"! And this helps you have closer relationships with the people around you.

The Penny Pitch Feelings Game on the next page can help you talk about your feelings and learn about the feelings of others. Play the game with anyone you like—a sibling, a parent, a friend, even someone you don't know very well. It will help you get to know them better!

Here's how to play:

1. Turn to the next page and flatten the book on a table **(or print the board from http://www.newharbinger.com/56029)**.

2. Collect enough pennies and give 5 coins to each player.

3. The youngest player goes first, takes a step back from the table, and tosses a coin at the page with the "feelings faces."

4. The player then talks about a time that they had that feeling.

5. When it comes to feelings, there are no right or wrong answers. Everyone who learns to understand their feelings is a winner!

Practice Being Mindful

Have you ever heard about being mindful? Being mindful is about paying attention to what's around you and what's happening. It's like shining a flashlight on what you are doing in a dark room. There are lots of other things in the room, but your focus is on wherever the flashlight is pointed.

Mindfulness is a very good skill to practice if you have ADHD. Sometimes teachers have students practice mindfulness because it can help them focus in class and keep calm. Practicing mindfulness regularly can help you do your schoolwork, homework, or other things that need all of your attention. Think of it as exercise for your brain.

On the next page, you'll find a picture of a bear walking in the woods to color. **(You can also download a copy from http://www.newharbinger.com/56029.)** Get a box of crayons and color in the picture. While you're coloring, be mindful. Breathe slowly, in and out. Focus on what you're doing, and use your senses. How does your crayon feel while you're coloring? Your fingers? Are you pressing your crayon down, and is it hard or soft? Look at how the picture changes as you color it. Notice how your body starts to relax as you color in the picture.

Color for about 10 minutes. If you start thinking about other things or want to get up and do something else, try to gently turn your mind back to your breathing and coloring. This is also being mindful.

Mindful coloring is a fun way to help you learn to focus. You can do it every day and also have a great collection of art!

Creating a Quiet Place

ACTIVITY 14

Sometimes things can get really busy. You have activities like sports or music lessons. You have homework and chores to do. And of course, you have to make time to play, and have some screen time, and explore outside.

But it's also important to find some quiet time. And this activity is about creating a place in your home to do just that.

Can you find just one spot in your home where you can go for 10 or 15 minutes each day for quiet time? Use the space below to think about what you would have in your quiet place and what you would do there.
You can draw what your quiet place looks like, or you can just write it down.

What would you put in your quiet place? Pillows? Stuffed animals? Books? Remember you can only put in things you can use quietly. **Draw or describe the things you could put in your quiet place.**

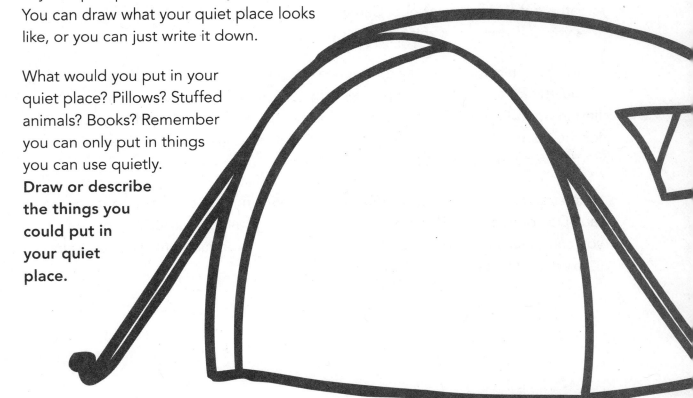

Shape Breathing

When you are upset about something, particularly if you are angry or frustrated, deep breathing can help.

It can also help if you are feeling fidgety and having a hard time focusing. When you are doing your homework or schoolwork, taking a break and practicing deep breathing for a few minutes can help you work for longer periods of time.

Sometimes we call deep breathing "belly breathing," because you breathe from your belly rather than your chest. Put your hand on your belly right now, and breathe in for a count of 5. Then hold your breath for the count of 2. Then breathe out for the count of 5. Can you feel your stomach rise and fall? Do you feel yourself starting to relax as you breathe?

Shape breathing is a fun way to practice deep breathing, relaxation, and focusing. Sit quietly for a minute and then, using the star on the next page, move your finger around the shape, breathing in for the count of 5, then holding your breath for the count of 2, and then breathing out for the count of 5. Do this as your finger traces the entire star.

When you are done going around the star, take a minute to think about how you feel. Do you feel calm? Do you feel relaxed? Do you feel focused? If you like, you can go around the star again, practicing your breathing until you feel calm, relaxed, and focused.

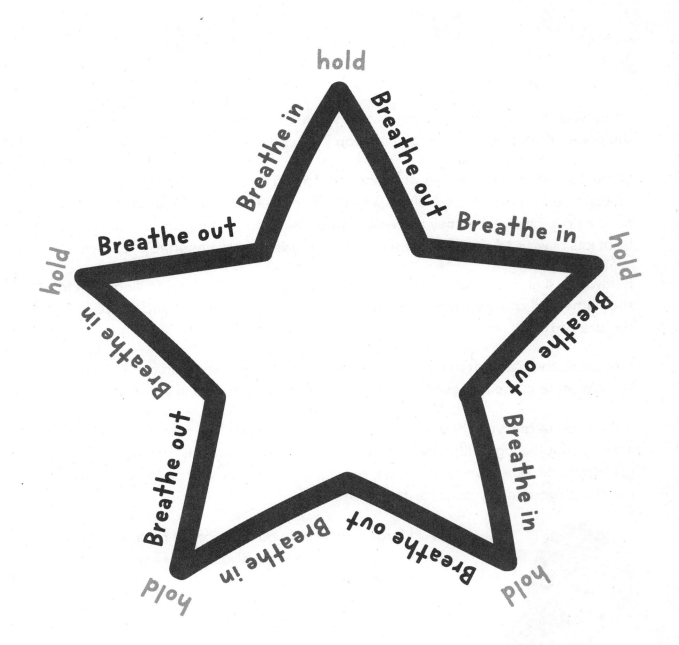

When You Have Difficult Feelings

Sometimes it's hard to ask for help when you are frustrated or upset or sad. But there are lots of people who can help you if you just ask.

Some kids may not realize that when they are feeling sad, frustrated, angry, or embarrassed, sharing these feelings will help them feel better. Others may even need help knowing what they are feeling. And when you ask for help, you can usually learn lots of ways to deal with the situations that give you uncomfortable feelings.

Below, you'll find questions about who can help you with different feelings. **Fill in the name and draw a picture of that person. You can also cut and paste in a picture of them.**

Of course, there are often many people who can help you with difficult feelings. You can write in the names of all the people who can help you, if you like.

Before you begin, you should think about the people you feel comfortable sharing your feelings with. These could be your parents, siblings, friends, grandparents, other family members, teachers, counselors, and clergy (people at the church your family goes to, if you go).

Did I forget any? I bet you have lots of people in your life who can help you learn about your feelings and solve problems you are facing.

48

Who can help you when
you are sad?

Who can help you when
you are angry?

Who can help you when
you are scared?

Who can help you when
you are frustrated?

Who can help you when
you are confused?

Who can help you when you are
feeling guilty about something?

Who can help you when
you are worried?

Who can help you when
you are irritated?

ACTIVITY 17

Where Do Your Feelings Come From?

Do you ever think about where your feelings come from? Feelings can come from lots of places.

Feelings come from experiences that you have. Think about how you feel when someone gives you an ice cream cone. Then think about how you feel when you are at the playground and it suddenly starts to rain.

Feelings can also come from the way that others treat you. Think about how you feel when someone you love gives you a hug. Think about how you feel when someone teases you or says something mean to you.

Feelings can even come from what you think about. Think about your last birthday party and the best present you got. How do you feel?

When you think about the things that make you feel good, you can do more of those things and feel good more of the time. When you think about the things that make you feel sad or upset, you can think about how to make these situations or thoughts better. You might want to talk to an adult about how to do this.

On the next page, you'll find some sentences about your feelings. **Finish the sentences to think about your different feelings and where they come from.**

I feel happy when

I feel sad when

I get excited when

I feel angry when

I feel scared when

I feel calm when

I feel proud when

I feel frustrated when

I feel loved when

I feel worried when

I feel hopeful when

I feel embarrassed when

Bonus!: Take one of the tougher feelings you wrote about. Maybe "sad," "angry," "scared," or "frustrated." **What's one way you can make the situation you wrote about better?**

Understanding How Others Feel

Probably the easiest way to understand someone else's feelings is to ask them "How are you feeling?" But people usually ask this question only when they see something about the other person that looks a little different. For example, your friend might have her head down on her desk. You might ask, "Is everything okay?" Or your dad might come home from work with a big smile on his face. You might ask, "Hey, Dad, why are you so happy?"

When we ask people about their feelings, it's usually because we are reading their nonverbal language. Nonverbal means "without words." Nonverbal language is what people show you by how they look or what they do, rather than what they say.

It takes a little practice to read nonverbal language, but a game of Feelings Charades can help. And it's a fun game too!

You can play with one other person or up to 6 people. Just cut out the feelings cards on the next two pages. **(You can also download the feelings cards from the website for this book, http://www.newharbinger.com/56029. Ask an adult for help with this.)** Then mix up the cards and put them in a pile.

The youngest player goes first and "acts out" the feeling on the card. That person can make different facial expressions or move their body any way they want. But they can't talk!

When someone guesses the right feeling, they get a point. If you want to learn more about nonverbal feelings, ask the person who guessed the correct answer to explain how they identified the feeling.

Then the next oldest player takes a turn.

Play for 15 to 30 minutes and the player with the most points is declared the winner.

SAD	ANGRY	PROUD
EMBARRASSED	GUILTY	SHY
AFRAID	BRAVE	SURPRISED
WORRIED	HAPPY	LOVING
JEALOUS	LONELY	SILLY
STRESSED	CALM	EXCITED
BORED	HURT	GRATEFUL
IRRITABLE	SHOCKED	SURPRISED

Print this page at
http://www.newharbinger.com/56029

More Than One Feeling at a Time

Often we act as if we feel only one way. But many times, we have different feelings about the same thing. For example, Tanya was excited to go over to her friend's house for a sleepover. But this was her first sleepover. So, she was nervous that she would miss her room, her toys, and her parents.

Part of learning to understand your feelings involves recognizing that you can have two or more feelings about the same thing. And that sometimes these feelings are the complete opposite of each other!

Look at the 4 children below and read about their situation. Then, write in different feelings that they might have about each situation.

MY MOM JUST HAD A NEW BABY.

57

MY DAD SAID WE CAN'T GO TO DISNEYLAND FOR A VACATION, BUT WE CAN GO TO THE BEACH.

MY FRIEND DROPPED AND BROKE MY CELL PHONE, BUT SHE IS GOING TO REPLACE IT.

I ONLY GOT A B ON MY TEST, BUT MY TEACHER SAID IT WAS THE BEST GRADE IN THE CLASS.

Now, think about situations where you have two different feelings about something important to you.

SITUATION:

SITUATION: _____

SITUATION: _____

Things That Are Great About You!

Kids with ADHD often hear about all the things they should do differently. They should sit quietly. They should study harder. They should be better at following directions. They should be more patient.

That's a lot of "shoulds" to think about.

It's important for kids with ADHD to also think about all the great things they can do. The things that make them very special, like drawing, or playing sports, or being funny, or being kind to others.

What are some things you really like about yourself? Write them down in the clouds below. If you run out of clouds, you can write the rest of your things right into the sky.

61

64

Thinking Ahead

Has anyone ever told you to "think before you act"? Have you ever thought about why this is important?

Joshua ran to the bus stop to go to school. There were dark clouds in the sky, but he didn't take a jacket or an umbrella. What do you think happened?

Shara's mother told her to never put a wet glass on their new wooden table because it would leave a ring that wouldn't come out. But Shara was drinking a glass of juice when she heard her phone go off, and she put the glass on the table while she went to get it. What do you think happened?

Jorge wanted to buy his mother her favorite perfume for her birthday. But whenever he got his allowance, he would spend it on buying new pieces for his collection of toy cars. Now it's just one week until his mother's birthday and he has only 2 dollars saved up. What do you think happened?

Have you ever had a problem because you didn't think ahead? Write what happened here:

You can learn to think ahead. You can learn to imagine what might happen in a situation, based on what you do or don't do, and use that to decide what you'll actually do. And you can avoid many problems if you can remember to do this. **What would help you remember to think before you act?**

Thinking ahead also takes some practice. **See how you can think ahead to solve the maze on the next page.**

Bobby needs to go home as quickly as he can to feed his dog, Finn. But if he takes the wrong path, it will take him longer. Draw the quickest path to help Bobby get home. Look ahead and try to avoid any paths that lead to a dead end.

See Answer Key on page 152.

Organizing Your Work

If you go to school, you probably have homework. If you have homework, you probably do it at a desk. And if you have a desk, it's important for that desk to be organized. You should have only the things you need on your desk and not things that will distract you.

Below, you'll find some scrambled words. Unscramble them. Then, put a circle around the things that will help you with your homework. You can add additional items too. On the next page, draw the items that you think you should have on and in your desk to help you with your work.

NEPSILC __ __ __ __ __ __ __

EPNS __ __ __ __

SNCRYAO __ __ __ __ __ __ __

PEPRA __ __ __ __ __

BOKO __ __ __ __

MORPEUTC __ __ __ __ __ __ __ __

SMAEKRR __ __ __ __ __ __ __

LCKOC __ __ __ __ __

KOMHOREW __ __ __ __ __ __ __ __

ETGDIF TYO __ __ __ __ __ __ __ __ __

See Answer Key on page 152.

List other items that you would want to help you with your homework:

_____

_____

NOW, DRAW THE ITEMS YOU NEED ON YOUR DESK TO DO YOUR HOMEWORK

HERE, DRAW ITEMS YOU MIGHT WANT IN YOUR DRAWERS

Paying Attention to Time

How do you feel about time? Kids like you (and adults too!) can find it hard to manage time. They can struggle to figure out whether they'll be early or late, or how to be efficient with what they do so they can finish the things they need to do.

For example, Daniel was always late. He often missed the bus for school and even the bus going home. He was late handing in his homework or getting to the dinner table. He was even late when it was time to do something fun, like going to the playground.

His twin sister, Dania, was always on time. If she was ever late, she got very upset, so she usually made sure to be 10 minutes early.

Which person are you more like—Daniel or Dania?

In this activity, you'll think about how good you are at estimating time by thinking about how long things take. For example, how long do you think your homework usually takes? Write your answer in the watch to the left. Then, the next time you do homework, use a watch or clock to track your time, and write how long it actually takes in the watch on the right. Finally, figure out how close your guess was to how long it actually took. Write the difference on the line.

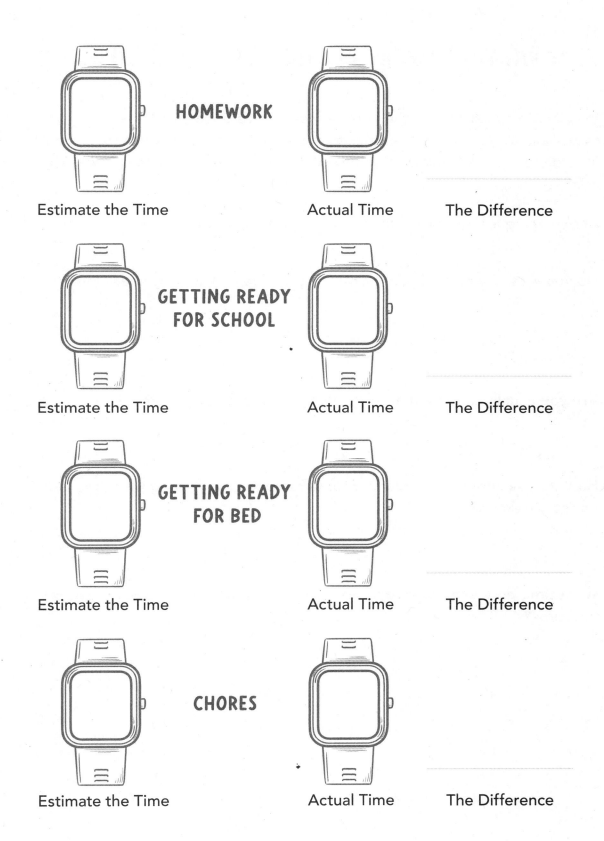

WHAT IS YOUR RELATIONSHIP WITH TIME?

We all have a relationship with time. Sometimes it's good: We know how long things will take us, and we can stick to a schedule when we need to. Sometimes it's a bit tougher: We might struggle with lateness or to complete the tasks we're asked to complete.

Answer the questions below to learn more about your relationship with time:

Do you wear a watch? If your answer is yes, does it have any special features?

Are you usually on time, late, or early when going to school?

How do you know when it's time to wake up in the morning for school and on the weekend?

What time do you go to bed at night? Why is it important to go to bed at that time?

When was the last time you were late for something? What happened?

Is there something you are always on time for?

Have you ever had to wait a long time for someone else? What happened?

Why do you think it's important to be on time?

If you want to be on time more often, what are some things you can do?

My Weekly Goals

A goal is something you want to achieve because it's very important to you. There are short-term goals and long-term goals, and they are both important.

For example, Andy wanted to learn to play the guitar. He wants to be in a rock band when he gets older. That's a long-term goal. He also wanted to learn to play a song he really liked for his school's talent show. That's a short-term goal. You can think of a short-term goal as something you can accomplish in the next day, week, or even month. A long-term goal is something you might achieve in a year or more.

Sometimes you can have short-term goals that are important by themselves, like getting an A on a spelling test. But when you have long-term goals, you usually have short-term goals that lead up to it. For instance, Andy's long-term goal—being in a rock band when he's older—might mean he needs to achieve some short-term goals, like taking lessons and practicing a couple times a week to build his skills and confidence.

On the next page, you'll find a worksheet on making weekly goals. **You can also find a printable copy of this worksheet at http://www.newharbinger. com/56029 (if you'd like to start a habit of setting goals).**

You can begin by listing some of the goals you might want to work on:

SHORT-TERM GOALS	LONG-TERM GOALS

MY GOALS

Your Goal: _____

Is this a short-term or long-term goal? _____

Why is this goal important? _____

_____

Steps to take: _____

_____

_____

_____

_____

What obstacles will you face? _____

_____

_____

How can you overcome these obstacles? _____

_____

Who can help you achieve your goal? _____

_____

Print this page at
http://www.newharbinger.com/56029

ACTIVITY 25

Making Good Choices

Every day you have many choices to make.

Some choices are easy to make. For example, Karl had a snack after school every day. He always chose his favorite fruit and nut bar.

Some choices you have to think about. Ling's parents let her choose doing her homework before or after dinner. She decided to do it as soon as she came home from school because then she wouldn't have to worry about getting it done.

Some choices can be hard to make. Kyle accidentally knocked over a table at his grandmother's house and a glass of soda fell on the rug. He put the table upright and picked up the glass, but he didn't know whether to tell his grandmother about it, because she might be mad. Kyle decided that he should tell her, and she wasn't mad at all.

Below are 10 choices that different kids have to make. For each situation, write down what you would do. Then, put a letter in the box for each choice to indicate whether you think the choice is easy (E), needs some thought (T), or would be hard for you to make (H).

E=Choice is easy
T=Choice needs some thought
H=Choice is hard

___ Ben was in a hurry. He thought he might skip washing his hands before dinner and no one would ever know. What would you do if you were Ben?

___ Nate didn't do his homework. The teacher has just asked him to hand in his assignment. What should he do?

___ Aaliyah wasn't tired. She thought she would watch YouTube videos even though it was a school night. What should she do?

___ Connor was afraid to try out for the basketball team because he thought he wasn't good enough to make the team. What would you tell him?

___ Olivia's friend Marcy was in the hospital, but Olivia didn't really want to visit her there. She was afraid Marcy would be upset. What would you do if you were Olivia?

___ Ethan had to choose a book for a book report. What book would you choose?

___ Madison didn't understand his math homework, but his mother said she was too busy to help him for another hour. What would you do if you were Madison?

___ Jasmine wanted to get a gift for her father's birthday, but she had only 2 dollars. What would you do in this situation?

___ Mia left her lunch box on the school bus. She didn't realize it until it was time to eat lunch. What would you do if you were her?

___ Zach saw his friend Ben take a candy bar from the store without paying for it. What would you do in this situation?

Remembering What Comes Next

Tim never seemed to get things completely done. Sometimes, he forgot about finishing them when he was halfway through. Like the time he was cleaning his room, but he got bored and went to play a video game. He thought he would finish cleaning later, but he didn't, and his dad was mad at him.

Sometimes, Tim would forget certain parts of what he was supposed to do. One morning, when he was getting ready for school, he put his books and computer in his backpack, but he forgot to pack the lunch his dad had made for him. His dad had to come to school and bring his lunch. He wasn't too happy about that either.

Sometimes, Tim would forget things completely! One Monday, as he was eating breakfast, he said, "I think I was supposed to be working on a science project about the weather." "When were you supposed to be doing that?" his mother asked with a frown.

"I think it was last week. Maybe. I'm not sure." What do you think his mother said about that?

Many kids with ADHD have trouble remembering things. This makes it harder for them to get things done on time and to follow the rules at home and at school. But even if you have a hard time remembering things, you can work on developing a better memory.

On the next page, take a look at the 12 things that Tim had to remember. Then, on the page after that, see how many you can remember by drawing them in the boxes. If you have to go back and look at the pictures once or twice, that's okay, but see if you can try to do it with just 1 or 2 looks.

 Do the dishes

 Be on time for dinner

 Put on sunscreen

 Make the bed

 Set the table

 Pack the backpack

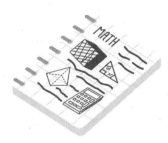 Do homework

 Pick up toys

 Drink water

 Take out the trash

 Be on time for breakfast

 Feed the dog

80

WHAT CAN HELP YOU REMEMBER?

If you have a difficult time remembering things, there are several things that can help. **Circle the ones that you think would be helpful to you and give them a try!**

Use a notebook to keep track of things.

Put a sticky note by the places where you have to remember important things.

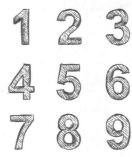

Use a calendar to keep track of important events.

Think about how many steps you have to take when doing a task and remember that number to make sure you do them all.

Making a Plan

A lot of things you do will be easier if you make a plan. A plan is like a treasure map. Imagine if you were trying to find buried treasure in the woods. If you didn't have a map, you would just wander around trying to figure out where to start. But with a map, you would just follow the path right to the treasure.

The activity on the next 2 pages will walk you through making a plan to help you achieve a goal. You'll start by making a plan to get a gift for someone you care about. Then you can make a plan for anything you want. Your goal is probably not going to get you buried treasure, but you should think of something very valuable to you.

Here are the steps to making a plan:

- Figure out what you need. What's your goal—the thing you want to get done?

- List the steps you need to take to reach your goal.

- Check the steps—your plan—to make sure it's complete.

- Follow your plan.

- Change your plan if you need to. You might find that you need to take a different step than the one you first decided on.

- Be proud of achieving your goal!

Your goal: **Buy a gift for a friend or relative**

List what you need:

List the steps to take:

- ☐ Check your plan.

- ☐ Are all the steps you'll need to take there?

- ☐ Are they in the right order?

- ☐ Follow your plan.

Make changes to your plan (if needed). Write them down here.

Now, it's time to make your own plan for a goal you're hoping to achieve, or something you know you'll need to get done. **You can download this goal planner at http://www.newharbinger.com/56029 if you'd like to use it for more goals.** We've added two on the following pages to get you started.

Your goal: _____

List what you need:

List the steps to take:

☐ Check your plan.

☐ Are all the steps you'll need to take there?

☐ Are they in the right order?

☐ Follow your plan.

Make changes to your plan (if needed). Write them down here.

Print this page at
http://www.newharbinger.com/56029

Your goal: _____

List what you need:

_____

_____

List the steps to take:

_____

_____

_____

_____

_____

_____

☐ Check your plan.

☐ Are all the steps you'll need to take there?

☐ Are they in the right order?

☐ Follow your plan.

Make changes to your plan (if needed). Write them down here.

_____

_____

_____

_____

Learning to Be Patient

It's not easy to be patient: to learn to be calm, to put up with things that frustrate you without getting upset, or to wait for something that's taking longer than you thought it would. But sometimes that's your only choice.

Are you a patient person? Circle one: YES   NO   SOMETIMES

What do you do when you have to be patient? Do you daydream? Think about something else? Talk to someone? Or something else?

Below are 6 times or places you need to be patient. On the next page, you'll find a crossword puzzle to fill in these times or places. You can use the pictures and the descriptions to help you fill in the places and times you need to be patient.

86

Down

1. A place where you have to wait for your meal

4. What you see at a theater

Across

2. You wait here to get on a roller coaster

3. It comes just once a year

5. A place where you have to wait your turn to talk

6. A place where flowers and vegetables grow

See Answer Key on page 153.

Keep Trying Even If It's Hard

Many times, you will have to do things that are hard. Maybe it's your homework, studying for a test that is coming up, or chores that you really don't like to do. Doing things that are hard is something we all have to do. This game will help you think of different things you can do to complete a task no matter how hard it is.

GAME INSTRUCTIONS

The goal of this game is to be the first person to win 10 points by finishing a difficult task.

What you need:

- 2 players

- 2 coins

- Die (use one from another game or make your own using the next page)

- Scorecard

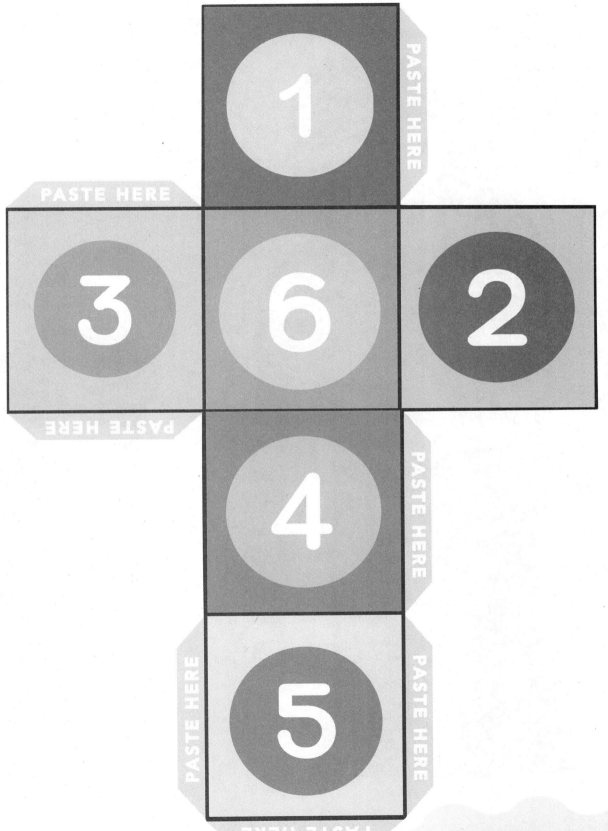

Print this page at
http://www.newharbinger.com/56029

How to play:

1. The younger player goes first and describes a difficult task they are working on. Both players will think about this task when they answer questions about obstacles. Then they roll the die.

2. Players can move their coin in any way that will get them the most points. They can move horizontally or vertically, but not diagonally.

3. Write down the points for each player on the scorecard on page 95.

4. When players reach an obstacle, they must describe a way to overcome that obstacle and continue working. They get 2 points for their answer.

5. When players have at least 5 points, they will try and get to the finish line and get another 5 points.

6. The first person to get 10 points is the winner.

7. At the end of the game, take a few minutes to talk about ways to keep working even when it's hard to do.

GAME 1

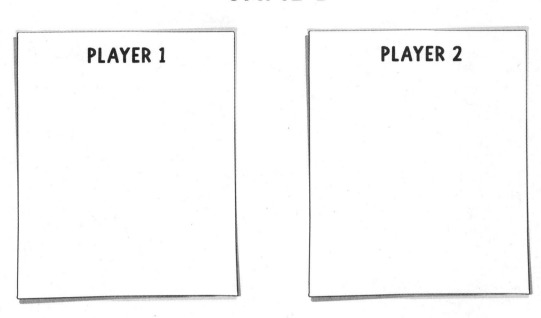

GAME 2

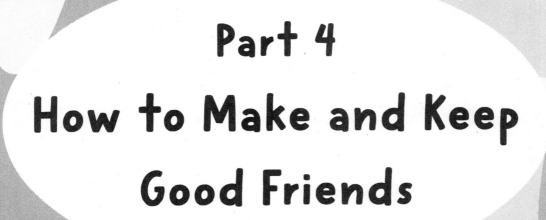

Part 4
How to Make and Keep Good Friends

How to Find Good Friends

It's great to have good friends to play with, to talk to, and to share experiences and adventures with. But sometimes it's hard to make friends.

Making new friends can take a little effort, but it's an effort that will pay off for many years to come. When you're trying to make a new friend, start by thinking about kids you know who enjoy the same things.

On the next page, you will find pictures of activities that kids enjoy. **Unscramble the words at the bottom of the page.** (Hint: The first letter of each activity is in bold and the scrambled words can be remixed to make 1 or 2 unscrambled ones.) **When you've unscrambled all the words, draw a line to match each one to its picture.**

97

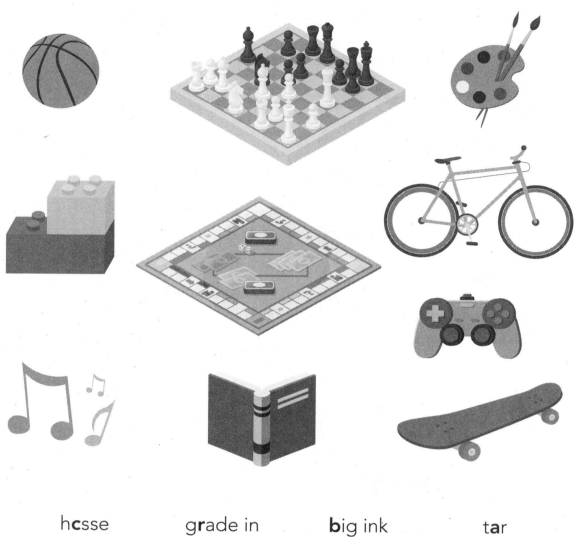

See Answer Key on page 153.

Now, here are some questions about how to make good friends for you to think about. Have fun!

Do you have a best friend? Who is it?

What do you like to do with your friends?

What would you say to someone who you thought might be a friend?

How do you know when someone is friendly?

What activities would you do with a new friend?

How do you know if someone doesn't want to be your friend?

How would you like your friends to act with you?

Do you treat your friends the same way you'd like them to treat you?

ACTIVITY 31
Making Time for Friends

Having friends is an important part of growing up, but some kids have a hard time fitting time with friends into a busy schedule. This activity will help you think about doing things with your friends that you will all enjoy.

Begin by talking to your parents about your friends (or kids you would like to have as friends). Your parents will probably want to know where they live, how to contact their parents, what they like to do, and more. Then, with your parents, plan some playdates. Fill in the information below for each playdate.

Name _____ **Date** _____

Activity _____

_____

Name _____ **Date** _____

Activity _____

_____

Name _____ **Date** _____

Activity _____

_____

Learning to Cooperate

Many things are easier when you cooperate. And they are more fun too! Lifting something heavy is easier. Playing soccer is more fun. Carrying in the groceries is easier. Playing a board game is more fun. Some things are impossible to do if you don't cooperate! Have you ever tried to play on the seesaw by yourself?

This game will show how good you are at cooperating. It's like the game of Pin the Tail on the Donkey, but instead you have to draw the tail on the animal. Here's how to play:

1. Find someone to play with you. It could be another child or a grown-up. You will also need a pen or pencil for this game.

2. You go first, and pick an animal. Look carefully at the tail because you will have to draw it from memory.

3. Now, get something to cover your eyes, like a scarf.

4. While your eyes are covered, the other player must tell you where to put your pen or pencil down on the picture of the same animal without a tail, and then you should draw the tail from memory.

5. If the tail is close to where it should be, you both get 1 point.

6. If the tail you drew also looks like the tail from that animal, you both get 2 points!

7. Now, switch places, and the other person puts on the blindfold while you help them draw a tail on another animal.

ACTIVITY 33

You Can Be a Leader

How many leaders do you know? The president is a leader of the country. Your principal is the leader of your school. A sports team has a leader called a captain. Companies like McDonald's or Disney have leaders called Chief Executive Officers (CEOs).

How about the kids you know? Who is a leader in your class? How about in your neighborhood?

A leader is someone who often makes decisions for the whole group. Those decisions are based on thoughts from the people in the group. A good leader makes sure that everyone who wants to share their idea gets to speak, and everyone else listens while they do. If there is a problem, the leader helps solve it by talking and listening to others.

Do you want to be a leader? You can start by learning the things that leaders do almost every day.

On the next page, you'll see signs that Emma's friends made to help her get elected as class president. Some of them talk about her leadership skills, but others don't. Circle only the signs that talk about her leadership skills. Put an "X" over the other signs.

Now, look at the leadership skills you circled on Emma's signs. On the next page, make leadership signs for yourself. You can also add any other leadership skills you think you have.

105

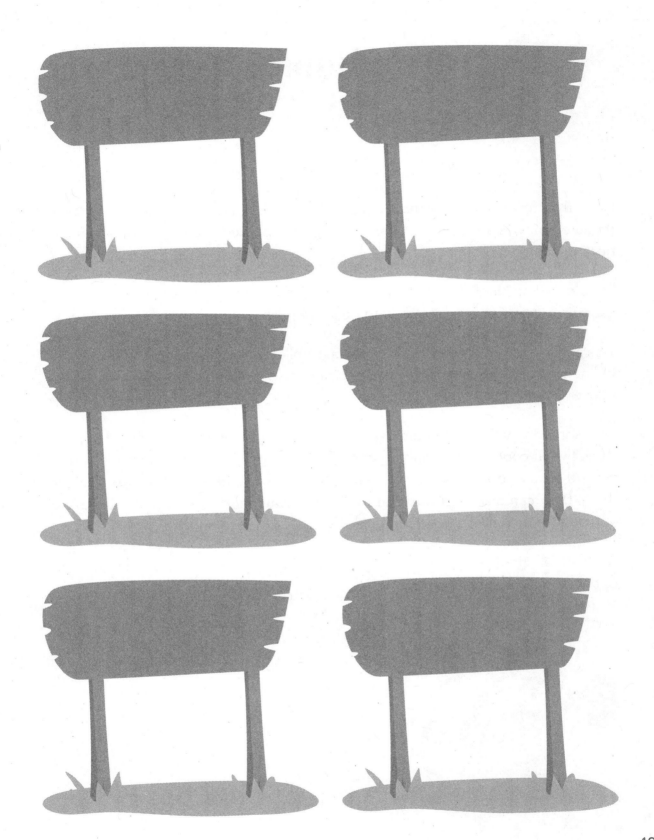

Be a Humor Detective

ACTIVITY 34

Do you laugh every day or maybe many times a day? Humor (laughing at things that are funny) is an important part of life and in particular an important part of getting along with others.

People love to laugh together, and laughing together helps people connect. Laughing together is a great way to build friendships.

This activity will help you laugh (or at least smile) with other people you know. It will help you be a humor detective—someone who can find laughter whenever they want.

Find someone you can share these pages with to practice being a humor detective. It could be an adult or someone your age. The first page has some areas the other person should fill in. The second page has questions you can ask them. (**You can also find these at http://www.newharbinger.com/56029.** Ask an adult for help if you need it.)

You can tell them you are practicing being a humor detective and trying to find out what makes people laugh.

Jokes are always fun (even if they are not always funny). Rate these jokes using this scale:

1 = not funny at all   2 = a little funny   3 = very funny

Why did the scarecrow win an award?

Because he was outstanding in his field!

Why did the bicycle fall over?

Because it was two-tired!

What do you call a bear with no teeth?

A gummy bear!

Add your own joke below.

Draw a picture of something silly.

Print this page at
http://www.newharbinger.com/56029

Describe a movie scene or a YouTube video you thought was really funny.

_____
_____
_____

Make a funny face!

Say one of these tongue twisters 5 times:
- Betty's beagle barked and bounced beside the big blue barn.
- Silly Sally swiftly shoos seven silly sheep.
- Five flying frogs flip funny flops.

When was the last time you couldn't stop laughing?

_____
_____

Who is the funniest person you know? Why did you choose that person?

_____
_____

Joining Others at Play

One way to make new friends is joining kids already playing and having fun. But sometimes it can be hard to approach kids and make new friends.

Take a look at the kids playing in the picture below and then answer the questions on the next page, using the numbers to identify each of the kids. When you're ready, try out what you've learned with kids in your school or on a playground.

111

Here are some ways to join other children at play. **Look at each suggestion and then refer back to the picture and put in the number of the child that matches the description (there may be more than 1 answer):**

___ Talk to someone who is smiling.
Don't forget to smile too!

___ Talk to someone who is doing something you like to do.
What's your favorite game to play?

___ Use a conversation starter, like "Is this your favorite game?"
What's another thing you could say to start a conversation?

___ Offer to help someone out.
What would you do to help someone out?

___ Give a compliment to someone.
What would you say to make someone feel good?

___ Find someone who looks friendly.
What is it about them that looks friendly?

___ Ask someone if you can play with them?
How did you make this choice?

___ Who is a person you wouldn't want to approach?
How did you make that decision?

Solving Conflicts with Others

People have problems all of the time. Friends argue, parents argue, and siblings get mad at each other too. Arguing and disagreeing with someone is part of most relationships, but the important thing is how these conflicts are resolved.

This activity will help you think about the best things to do when you have a conflict with someone else. Even when you disagree with someone, you can act in a respectful way that can help solve a problem rather than make it worse.

On the next page are 8 ways to handle a conflict with someone else. Read them carefully and talk about them with an adult. You might want to practice them in a role-play, acting out a recent problem you had with a friend or relative.

It's important to remember these "conflict busters" so you can use them when you have a problem with someone else, and this word search can help you think about them and understand them better.

Find the word or words in bold on the word search. See if you can find all 8 without help. If you need help, you can check the answer key in the back of the book.

What is a recent problem that you had with a friend?

_____
_____
_____
_____
_____

What is a recent problem that you had with a relative?

_____
_____
_____
_____
_____

Here are some ways you can help avoid an argument:

- Show **empathy** by thinking about how the other person feels.
- Find a **compromise**, so the other person gets something they want.
- **Brainstorm** a solution to the problem, thinking of as many ways as you can to solve the conflict.
- State what you **need** and why you need it. Take a minute to **calm down** if you are upset. **Ask for help** from an adult if you need it.
- **Apologize** if you have done something that has upset the other person.
- **Stand up** for yourself in a polite way.

See Answer Key on page 154.

Understanding What Others Think and Feel

Do you know what empathy is? It means seeing things from another person's point of view and understanding how they feel. This is such an important thing to do!

When you pay attention to what others think and feel, you can act in ways that are helpful to them, and they will really appreciate it and probably let you know. Most importantly, when you understand others around you, you can act in ways that show you care.

Everyone is born with the ability to empathize with others, but sometimes we forget how important this is. If you need to be more empathetic, you can do this by paying careful attention to what people look like—their facial expressions and their body language. You can also listen to their voice. Do they seem angry, tired, or worried? Don't just listen to their words, but listen to the way they talk.

On the next two pages are 8 people who have different problems. **See if you can "put yourself in their shoes," and in each box, write what they are thinking and feeling.**

Tim broke his ankle playing basketball. **What is the hardest thing for Tim to do at school?**

_____

_____

Ms. Robbins, a teacher of 25 kids, came to school with a bad headache. **What do you think could make this headache better or worse?**

_____

_____

Mina's mother just went to the hospital. **What do you think she is thinking? What is she feeling?**

_____

_____

Josh was having a birthday party, but he was new to the school and wasn't sure whom to invite. **What do you think he was worried about?**

_____

_____

117

Mr. Henry works as a janitor in an elementary school. **What do you think he likes about his job? What do you think annoys him?**

_____

_____

Darius's house was destroyed by a flood. **What are his biggest concerns?**

_____

_____

Tanisha is going to have a new baby brother. **What do you think she's thinking about?**

_____

_____

Miguel overheard his parents arguing. They seemed really mad. **What do you think Miguel was thinking?**

_____

_____

Understanding Personal Space

The easiest way to understand your personal space is to take a hula hoop and get in the middle of it (or imagine you are in the middle of one). The space between your body and the hoop is your personal space.

Most of the time, particularly at school, people stand outside your personal space. They don't stand too close or touch you.

When you are with your family, you may have people in your personal space. Your mom or dad will hug you or kiss you good night. Your brother or sister or friends may get closer to you when you are playing.

Sometimes, a person might get close to you, and it can be a problem, even a danger. For example, a stranger should never be in your personal space for any reason. If a stranger touches you, you should walk away and tell an adult.

On the next page are situations of kids dealing with personal space issues. Circle the emoji that best describes how you might feel in each situation.

1. John's grandpa gave him a big hug when he came over for dinner.

2. Samuel saw that Ella was sitting by herself crying. He didn't know what was wrong, but he put his arm around her shoulders.

3. Tyrone, an older neighbor, asked Charise to sit on his lap.

4. Devon was fooling around on the playground and started wrestling with Charlie.

5. Luna always held hands with her sister when they went to the mall.

6. Grace punched Michael on the arm while they were in the line to go out for recess.

7. Eleanor thought it would be funny to tease Elijah by kicking his foot under the table.

8. Lucas was mad at his brother Patrick and pinched his arm as hard as he could.

9. Anna gave Lucy a high five after she scored the winning point in their basketball game.

10. Eric's dad was tickling him and he said "Stop!" even though he was laughing.

121

Part 5
Making the Most Out of School

Asking for Help with Your Schoolwork

Everyone needs help with their work some of the time. But a lot of kids don't know whom to ask for help.

Maybe you are not sure of the kind of help you need.

Maybe you are not sure whom to ask.

Maybe you are shy and don't like asking for help.

It's important to remember that you have lots of people in your life who want to help you be a good student, and all you have to do is ask!

Start by putting checks on the line next to people who can help you with your schoolwork. Then, use the next page to write about what you need. You can either give this sheet to someone who can help you or use it to think about what you will say. The important thing is to ask!

People who can help me:

___ A parent

___ My classroom teacher

___ Another teacher at my school

___ A relative

___ A tutor

___ Someone else _____

Name: _____

Today's date: _____ Time: _____

I need help with:

_____
_____
_____
_____

I'm feeling:

_____
_____
_____
_____

I think you could help me by:

_____
_____
_____
_____

Thank you!

Print this page at
http://www.newharbinger.com/56029

Using Notes to Remember Important Things to Do

ACTIVITY 40

Do you ever forget things that are important? What happens when you forget to do important things?

Quinn worked hard on their homework but then forgot to put it in their backpack. Their teacher said they would get a lower grade because their homework wasn't done on time.

Bodhi forgot to wash his hands before dinner and his mother frowned and she sent him back to the bathroom.

Alisha loved to play with Legos, but even though she knew she was supposed to put them away when she was through, she forgot and went outside to play basketball with her friends. When she came back home, her dad told her there would be consequences for not putting her Legos away.

Some kids find it easier to remember things when they write sticky notes and put them in places so that the notes will remind them.

On the next page are 4 places where kids often need reminders of what to do. **Write on each note what you would want to remember in those places.**

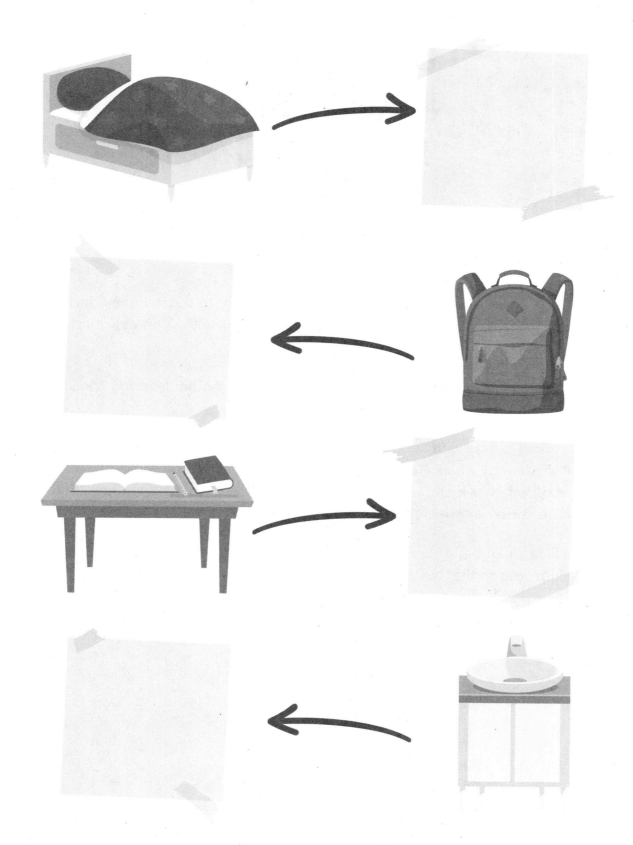

Knowing When to Take a Break

When you are doing homework, sometimes you need to take a break so that you can focus better. Below is a story about Chang, who knows that he gets distracted when doing his work. But he has learned that taking a break can help him finish his assignments on time. **Using your own experience, fill in the blank spaces to complete Chang's story about taking breaks.**

Hi! My name is Chang.

Sometimes, when I'm working on _____, I start to feel tired, frustrated, or fidgety.

My head starts to feel _____.

My body starts to feel _____.

I start to think _____.

When I start to feel this way, it means my brain and body need a break.

Taking _____ deep breaths can be a good break, particularly if relaxes my _____ at the same time.

Sometimes it helps if I stand up and stretch for _____ minutes. If I want to do this at school, I ask _____.

Using a fidget toy also helps me when I want to take a break. My fidget toy looks like _____.

After I take a break, the first thing I do is _____.

When I finish my work, I almost always feel _____.

129

Using Technology to Help with Your ADHD

Do you have a cell phone, tablet, or computer? If the answer is yes, then you probably already know that there are many different ways that technology can help you with ADHD.

There are many apps (short for applications) that can help you with your schoolwork and also with other challenges that you may have with ADHD.

This activity is designed to be filled in with a parent, teacher, or someone who knows how technology can be used to help kids with ADHD. Together, you can look up different apps and decide which ones might be helpful to you.

After you try an app out, you can rate it to see how helpful it was using the following scale:

1 = Not helpful at all

2 = Helpful some of the time

3 = Great!

Apps That Help You with Schoolwork

Apps That Turn Speech into Text

Apps That Keep a Schedule or Calendar

Mindfulness and Relaxation Apps

Timer Apps

Creative Expression Apps

Exercise and Movement Apps

Apps That Teach Social Skills

Apps That Improve Memory

Other Apps

Completing Homework Assignments

Homework might not always be fun, but it helps you in many ways.

When you do your homework, you do better in school and get better grades.

Doing your homework helps you get smarter. Each time you solve a math problem, write a story, or learn new words, your brain gets stronger.

Doing your homework isn't just about learning facts; it also helps you develop important work habits, like planning when to do things, trying even when work is hard, and finishing work on time.

Homework is an important way for you to show your parents and teachers how you can learn. When they see you completing your work on time, they know you're trying your best, which makes them happy and proud of you. If you're struggling with homework, they can see where you may need help to succeed.

Doing homework on time (and without a fuss) takes some practice, and the weekly planner on the next page can help.

Make a copy of the weekly homework planner on the next page **(or download it from http://www.newharbinger.com/56029)** and fill it out each day as you get homework assignments. In the "mood" column, draw an emoji of how you are feeling when you complete each assignment.

133

WEEKLY HOMEWORK PLANNER

MONDAY

ASSIGNMENT	DUE	DONE	MOOD
			◯
			◯
			◯

TUESDAY

ASSIGNMENT	DUE	DONE	MOOD
			◯
			◯
			◯

WEDNESDAY

ASSIGNMENT	DUE	DONE	MOOD
			◯
			◯
			◯

THURSDAY

ASSIGNMENT	DUE	DONE	MOOD
			◯
			◯
			◯

FRIDAY

ASSIGNMENT	DUE	DONE	MOOD
			◯
			◯
			◯

Print these pages at
http://www.newharbinger.com/56029

Preparing for a Test

Do you worry about getting a good grade on your tests?

Getting good grades is like finding buried treasure—it helps when you have a good map! There are 7 steps that can help you study for tests. These steps are described below, and you can also find them on the next page. As you do each step, make your way through the maze to get to the treasure chest:

Step 1: Make a study plan before. Look at a calendar with your parents and decide which days you will study and how much you will study. For example, if your test is on Friday, you could study for 20 minutes each day starting on Monday. This way, you don't have to study everything all at once, and you'll have plenty of time.

Step 2: Gather your materials. Make sure you have everything you need before you start (books, notes, pencils, and anything else). This way, you won't have to get up and search for things while you're trying to concentrate.

Step 3: Find a quiet place. It's easier to focus when it's quiet, so find a spot where you won't be distracted. It could be your bedroom, the kitchen table, or even a corner in your living room. Make sure there's good light, and you have a comfortable chair to sit in.

Step 4: Break it down into steps. Instead of trying to study everything at once, break what you have to learn into smaller pieces. Smaller chunks can make learning more manageable. A parent, caregiver, or teacher can help you do this. For example, if you have to learn 10 spelling words, try learning 3 or 4 words at a time. Once you know them, move on to the next group.

Step 5: Plan short breaks. Your brain works better when it has a chance to rest. After about 15 to 20 minutes of studying, take a 5-minute break. Make a plan about what kind of breaks will be helpful (see activity 43 to learn about taking breaks).

Step 6: Review what you learned. At the end of your study time, quickly go over what you learned. This will help your brain remember everything when you need it. You can ask a parent or friend to quiz you, or you can teach what you learned to someone else.

Step 7: Get a good night's sleep. The night before your test, make sure you get plenty of sleep. A good night's rest will help your brain be ready to do its best work.

Name of the Test _____

Date of the Test _____

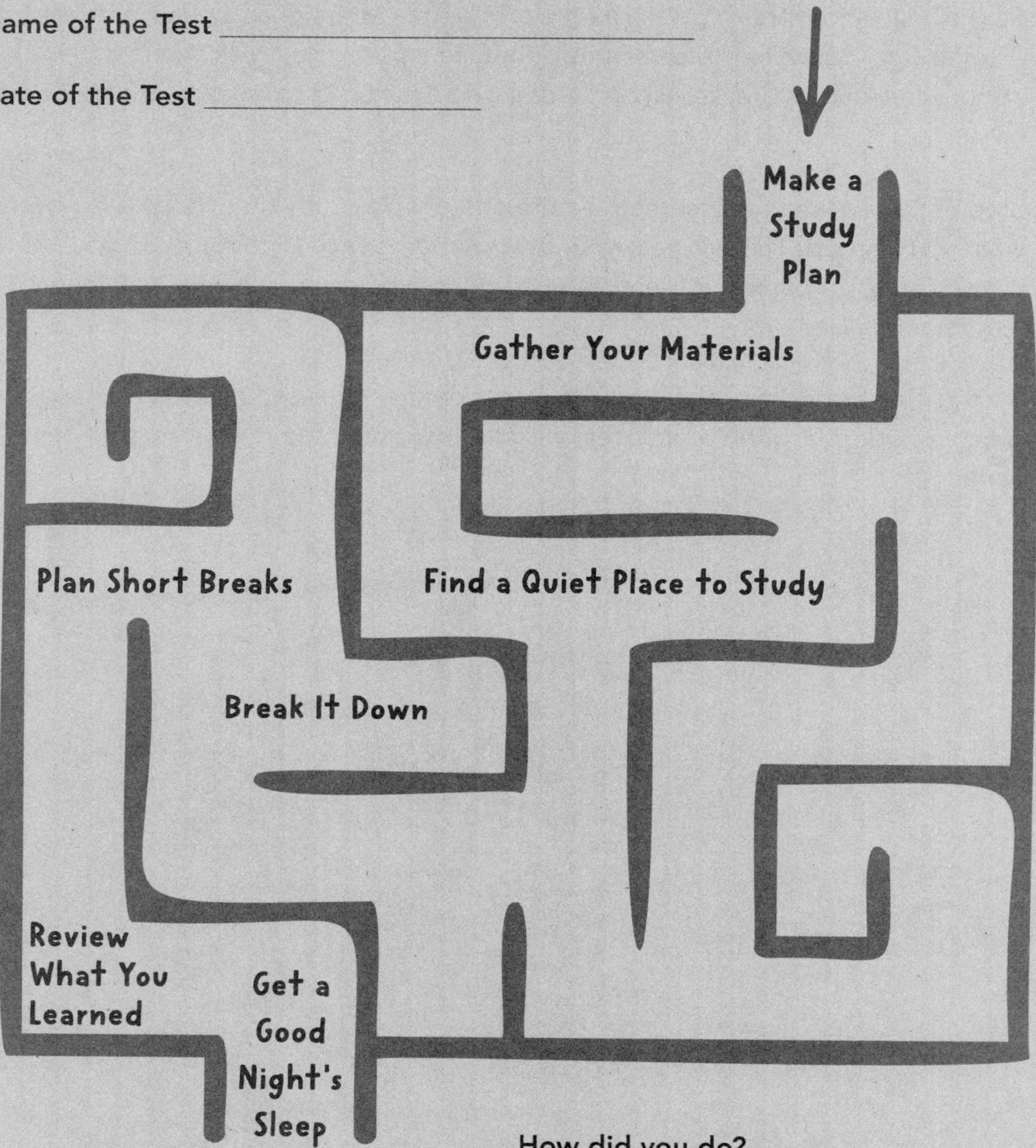

Make a Study Plan

Gather Your Materials

Plan Short Breaks

Find a Quiet Place to Study

Break It Down

Review What You Learned

Get a Good Night's Sleep

How did you do?

_____

_____

_____

Speaking in Front of the Class

Few kids like to speak in front of the class, but we all need to do it at some time. It might be scary, but the more you practice, the easier it will be. Maybe it always feels hard, but you'll know that you've done it before, so you can do it again.

Speaking in public will be even more important as you get older. You'll have more presentations to do in school. When you have a job, you might need to share your ideas in groups, lead projects, or explain important things. When you learn to speak your mind, organize what to say, and say it clearly in front of others, it becomes easier to work in teams and solve problems.

Speaking in front of a class is also a way to show your personality. You get to explain something with your words, and that makes you unique.

On the next page is a checklist that will show you steps to prepare to speak in front of your class. On page 141 is a picture of a pretend class.

When you have completed all the steps, practice talking in front of this pretend class. You can also use this checklist to prepare for any presentations you're assigned in school. **Visit http://www.newharbinger.com/56029 to download it.**

CHECKLIST

☐ Write down the topic you'll be speaking on.

_____

_____

☐ Write the amount of time you will be speaking.

_____

☐ Learn everything you can about the topic you will be talking about.

☐ Practice just talking about the topic with a parent or other adult. They should wait until you are done before asking questions.

☐ Write down the main points you want to make on index cards. You can use these when you practice, and your teacher may let you use them while you are speaking.

☐ If it's okay with your teacher, create visual aids to go along with your speech. Visual aids are pictures, drawings, or simple props, and these can help you focus your speech and make you feel more comfortable while speaking.

☐ Set a timer and practice your speech in front of the pretend class on the next page.

Remember that the more you practice, the easier it will be to speak in front of your class or anywhere else!

Print this page at
http://www.newharbinger.com/56029

Following Directions in School

Sophia had a hard time listening in school, even when her teacher was giving important directions.

Her teacher, Mr. Jones, reminded her that when you don't listen to directions, things can go wrong and it can even be dangerous. On the next 2 pages are things that Mr. Jones told the class. **In the boxes beside each direction, write about what might happen if Sophia doesn't follow each direction.**

"Bring lunch money for the school trip."

"Line up quietly and quickly when you hear a fire alarm."

"Wait your turn to use the playground equipment."

"Focus on your own work when doing independent reading."

"Study tonight for the quiz tomorrow."

"Raise your hand when you want to speak."

Hidden Rules at School

There are lots of rules kids have to follow, particularly at school. There are 2 types of rules—what teachers call "written rules" and "hidden rules."

You might find written rules anywhere in your classroom. Some teachers write rules on the board and some teachers have rules written on a poster.

Here are some examples of rules that teachers write down:

- Raise your hand to speak.

- Keep your hands and feet to yourself.

- When you are asked to line up, do it quietly and quickly.

But there are also hidden rules at school. These are rules that your teacher may not write down, but they are still important rules on how to behave, particularly with other people. Examples of hidden rules are:

- Be polite by saying "please" and "thank you."

- Help others without being asked.

- Don't stare at other people.

Hidden rules can be just as important as written rules, so it's important to know them.

On the next page, you'll see 5 written rules for the classroom. Write down 5 more important written rules in your class.

WRITTEN RULES

Add 5 more rules that are important in your school.

1. Do not make fun of other kids or tease them.
2. Listen when someone else is talking.
3. Ask for permission to leave the classroom.
4. Respect others' belongings—ask before touching and take only what's yours.
5. Keep your desk clean and throw away trash.
6.
7.
8.
9.
10.

HIDDEN RULES

Now, here are 10 hidden rules. Some of the words are scrambled up. You'll have to unscramble the words to understand each hidden rule. (Hint: The first letter in each word is in bold.)

Greet and me**s**il _____ at people in a dleif**n**ry _____ way.

Be ready to na**l**er _____ .

Say x**e**usce _____ me if you pmu**b** _____ into someone.

Keep your sy**e**e _____ on your own work.

Be usiru**c**o _____ and try new gih**t**sn _____ .

O**w**kr _____ together.

Use your inside oi**v**ec _____ in the classroom.

Stay veo**p**tisi _____ —we learn by making skati**m**es _____ .

Wait for a pause he**w**n _____ other people are knliag**t** _____ .

The answers are in the answer key in the back of the book.

See Answer Key on page 155.

The Gifts of ADHD

Have you heard about all the famous people who have or had ADHD? Many of these people found that the same qualities that caused problems when they were kids were actually "gifts" that made them stand out as adults.

This activity will teach you about six of these people, but many more people have ADHD and have become very successful because of these special gifts.

Read about these people on the next two pages and then think about how you might use these same gifts as you grow up. Do you know adults who have ADHD? Maybe you could ask them about how the gifts of ADHD have helped them as they grew up.

147

RISK TAKER

Before he created Mickey Mouse, Walt Disney struggled as a student, went bankrupt, and failed as an actor. But whatever challenge he faced, he used his highly creative mind to keep starting over again and trying new ideas. Now he's known as the creator of many beloved characters and Disney theme parks, and his imagination and business ideas will never be forgotten.

What new things have you tried?

HIGHLY FOCUSED

Simone Biles was diagnosed with ADHD at a young age. Like many children with the condition, she initially faced challenges in school and in her early gymnastics training. The structured environment of her training and the encouragement of her coaches kept her going and she never quit. Her focus on and passion for gymnastics helped her win 11 Olympic medals.

What are some things that help you do your best?

ENERGETIC

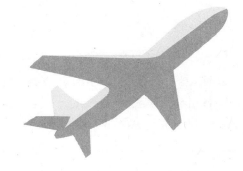

Founder of the Virgin Group, Richard Branson is a businessman known for his boundless energy and enthusiasm. Diagnosed with ADHD, Branson has built an empire through his ability to channel his high energy into multiple businesses at once.

What do you like to do when you feel your energy?

SPONTANEOUS AND FUNNY

Jim Carrey, the comedic actor known for his highly spontaneous and flexible performances, exemplifies this ADHD trait. His improvisational skills and unpredictable style have made him one of the most dynamic performers in Hollywood, and his willingness to embrace change and spontaneity has been key to his success.

What is the funniest thing you ever did?

CURIOUS

Leonardo da Vinci, often considered one of the most curious minds in history, was constantly seeking new knowledge across fields like anatomy, engineering, and art. Though ADHD was not recognized in his time, his diverse interests and curiosity reflect ADHD traits. Da Vinci's notebooks are filled with unfinished ideas and sketches, a hallmark of someone whose curiosity drove him from one idea to the next.

What are you curious about?

CREATIVE

Dav Pilkey is the creator of Captain Underpants, Dog Man, and many other popular books for kids. When he was young, Dav Pilkey's hyperactivity got him into trouble, but that didn't keep him from spending time writing stories and drawing pictures. He has said that his ADHD helped fuel his imagination to write stories that were creative and interesting to others.

What creative thing do you love to do?

Answer Key

Activity 6 Helping Superheroes

Multiple answers are possible, but here are some. The giraffe could help Judy reach the can on the cupboard. The bear looks like someone Khalid could go running with. The rhino could help Keisha poke a hole in the wall. The bulldog or turtle could be a good friend for Journee.

Activity 7 Good Manners

Multiple answers are possible, but here are some: burping, eating with his mouth open, dirty shirt, eating with his hands, slurping, food is off the plate.

Activity 8 What to Say to Ask for Help

Multiple answers are possible.

Activity 9 Dealing with Distractions

1. Boy playing guitar
2. Water dripping from roof
3. Phone ringing
4. Baby crying
5. Two kids fighting with pillows
6. TV on
7. Bird squawking

8. Dog barking
9. Cat meowing
10. Roof leaking

Activity 21 Thinking Ahead

Activity 22 Organizing Your Work

Unscrambled words: pencils, pens, crayons, paper, book, computer, markers, clock, homework, fidget toy

Activity 28 Learning to Be Patient

Crossword answers:

1 Down: RESTAURANT
2 Across: LINE
3 Across: BIRTHDAY
4 Down: MOVIE
5 Across: CLASSROOM
6 Across: GARDEN

Activity 30 How to Find Good Friends

Unscrambled words: chess, reading, biking, art, music, skateboard, Legos, board games, video games, basketball

Activity 33 Useful Leadership Qualities

These qualities make Emma a good leader:

Emma keeps trying even when things are hard.

Emma is a good problem solver.

Emma is responsible.

Emma listens to what others think.

Emma is responsible.

Emma is confident.

Activity 36 Solving Conflicts with Others

Activity 47 Hidden Rules at School

Unscrambled rules:

Greet and smile at people in a friendly way.

Be ready to learn.

Say excuse me if you bump into someone.

Keep your eyes on your own work.

Be curious and try new things.

Work together.

Use your inside voice in the classroom.

Stay positive—we learn by making mistakes.

Wait for a pause when other people are talking.

Lawrence E. Shapiro, PhD, is a renowned and internationally recognized child psychologist known for his innovative play-oriented techniques. He has invented more than seventy-five therapeutic games used by therapists around the world, and is creator of the *Instant Help* series for kids. He has written more than sixty books for children, teens, parents, and mental health professionals. Together, his books have sold nearly half a million copies worldwide, and have been translated into twenty-eight languages.

MORE BOOKS from NEW HARBINGER PUBLICATIONS

MINDFULNESS FOR KIDS WITH ADHD

Skills to Help Children Focus, Succeed in School, and Make Friends

978-1684031078 / US $16.95

Instant Help Books
An Imprint of New Harbinger Publications

THE BIG BOOK OF BIG FEELINGS

An Emotional Intelligence Activity Book for Kids

978-1648484445 / US $16.95

Instant Help Books
An Imprint of New Harbinger Publications

THE ANXIETY BUSTING WORKBOOK FOR KIDS

Fun CBT Activities to Squash Your Fears and Worries

978-1648483257 / US $21.95

Instant Help Books
An Imprint of New Harbinger Publications

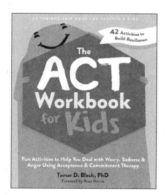

THE ACT WORKBOOK FOR KIDS

Fun Activities to Help You Deal with Worry, Sadness, and Anger Using Acceptance and Commitment Therapy

978-1648481819 / US $18.95

Instant Help Books
An Imprint of New Harbinger Publications

A WORKBOOK FOR KIDS WHO WORRY

Fun Activities to Help Children Face Their Fears and Build a Flexible Mindset Using Acceptance and Commitment Therapy

978-1648483424 / US $21.95

Instant Help Books
An Imprint of New Harbinger Publications

RAISING GOOD HUMANS

A Mindful Guide to Breaking the Cycle of Reactive Parenting and Raising Kind, Confident Kids

978-1684033881 / US $16.95

newharbingerpublications

1-800-748-6273 / newharbinger.com

(VISA, MC, AMEX / prices subject to change without notice)

Follow Us

Don't miss out on new books from New Harbinger.
Subscribe to our email list at **newharbinger.com/subscribe**